FALLING ILL

Books by C.K. Williams

POETRY
A Day for Anne Frank
Lies
I Am the Bitter Name
The Lark. The Thrush. The Starling. (Poems from Issa)
With Ignorance
Tar
Flesh and Blood
Poems 1963–1983
Helen
A Dream of Mind
New & Selected Poems
The Vigil
Repair
Love About Love
The Singing
Collected Poems
Creatures
Wait
Writers Writing Dying
All at Once
Selected Later Poems
Falling Ill

ESSAYS
Poetry and Consciousness
On Whitman
In Time: Poets, Poems, and the Rest

MEMOIR
Misgivings

TRANSLATIONS
Sophocles' Women of Trachis
    (with Gregory Dickerson)
The Bacchae of Euripides
Canvas, by Adam Zagajewski
    (translated with Renata Gorczynski and Benjamin Ivry)
Selected Poems of Francis Ponge
    (with John Montague and Margaret Guiton)

C.K. WILLIAMS

FALLING ILL

BLOODAXE BOOKS

Falling Ill: Last Poems by C.K. Williams

Copyright © 2016 by The Estate of C.K. Williams

Published by arrangement with Farrar, Straus and Giroux LLC,

18 West 18th Street, New York, NY 10011, USA. All rights reserved.

ISBN: 978 1 78037 355 3

This edition first published 2017 by
Bloodaxe Books Ltd
Eastburn
South Park
Hexham
Northumberland NE46 1BS

and by Farrar, Straus and Giroux in the US.

www.bloodaxebooks.com
For further information about Bloodaxe titles
please visit our website or write to
the above address for a catalogue.

Supported using public funding by
**ARTS COUNCIL
ENGLAND**

Cover design: Neil Astley & Pamela Robertson-Pearce

Printed in Great Britain by Bell & Bain Limited, Glasgow, Scotland, on
acid-free paper sourced from mills with FSC chain of custody certification.

For Catherine

Always

CONTENTS

Flame

From your workshop the usual commotion
the insistent exhalations of your torch
a hammer banging shy tings from silver

then your footsteps from one side of the room
to the other as though you were on a ship
checking the horizon for indolent dawn

then a long silence implying you must have
usurped a morsel of time to think of something
and priceless time waits to be certain you haven't

squandered anything of it in a tiny packet
an envelope with an hour still unspent then
time begins again then silence again

your door opening your footsteps on the stairs
and then the thought of you as your flame ignites
again and once more moves towards me again

Diagnosis

The sympathetic young woman doctor
informs me with an awkward uncharacteristic
formality that the laboratory has reported

not only on my blood but on the day's worth
of urine I'd amassed in a plastic bottle and
that I've been *diagnosed* awful word and that

I'm afflicted with a malady the name of which
I've never heard but which arrives now
in an alliterated appellation that sounds to me

utterly harmless what menace after all can
blameless alliteration contain and perhaps
that's why I find myself in spite of myself

blurting out *well that certainly makes things*
interesting no? that's what in my utter
witlessness came blurting *interesting no?*

Box

Volume I once believed of adhesive fragments
over which I presumed I'd always preside
but I'm informed has filled with renegade

somethings replacing the bits over which
I now assert nothing rather I'm more
a box in which amass insidious devourers

and when I picture myself I'm mostly
transparent not in the accusing greys of an x-ray
but in a substance something like what

was once called *spirit* imperceptible yet insistent
is it surprising then to imagine I might want
to flee from this box that heaves and groans

like a tree blasted by wind the cries of innocent
root twig and branch coursing through
this absence within me but no longer mine?

Heading Home

Now I'm a *hero* I think I might even be
a *star* I think or think I think *star*
for the first time in what's been merely a life

I say *think* because who can guess what you
postulate when your mortality distant or near
is proclaimed what do you do but stash

the news in the battered trunk of your ego
because you know that if you're the hero
the protagonist of this contest you'd scorn

such matters as death laugh at and about it
therefore this must be *theater* for isn't death
a *spectacle* and don't *stars* or *heroes* don't even

actors playing star-heroes always *prevail*
even if they don't appear to be paying attention
don't they still always carry the day?

Pops

Pops of pain here and there on my torso
and knee insistent though at first
unremarkable shots from some hidden bunker

and with them arrives the disquieting question
of whether they're the innocent pangs I've always
felt and dismissed or might they be indications

of something newly arrived to be received
with dread and what a trap that notion evokes
of having to admit the distractions

you've allowed yourself your whole life
are illusions and such a bizarre notion it is
too that you might lie to yourself as though

you truly could be the two-part invention
you conceived you'd made of yourself
just as it's all untuning all coming apart

My Body

I keep wandering away or rushing or bolting
or anyway fleeing for my life I suppose I'd say
from the truth that to speak now of *my body*

is absurd because doesn't my body possess
me hasn't my *me* succumbed so to my body
that I possess nothing in this realm of owning

and the real question is if my body possesses me
is it capable of speaking without my permission
and if so might that be what it's doing here

but then when would the *I* that used to seem
to exist apart from my body have its turn
if I'm my body's *me* or perhaps it's neither

my body nor me but my illness that speaks
that keeps seizing the chance to assert dominion
unless *(how not think this?)* it already has

Telling

I don't decide to tell or not tell you
I'm ill I don't decide to confess because
the notion of acknowledgment itself

becomes repugnant because it's so close
to something like accomplishment or pride
look what I have become being ill

sometimes to tell or not is a contest
a fruitless absurd struggle I might win
an agon in which I might overcome myself

to keep from divulging keep from squealing
as though making up my mind for such
a trivial thing had become a moral issue

and I come to feel I've degraded myself
and you and everything else with this spewing
this unthoughtout revelation of dismay

Next

Always I've been fixed on what comes next
what might be arriving or be on its way
next and after next and subsequent to that

but now it's gotten out of hand pathetic
nearly pathological I reach out compulsively
towards it whatever it is dwell on it and

not just dwell but allow myself to be bound
by it or in it I enter this 'next' as into
some elaborate structure where I imagine

a nest in which one might repose and ponder
except I don't ponder I generate thoughts
whose shape I'm unable to determine so I'm left

with next only next in which I move purpose to
purpose while knowing I'm only keeping track
that my future tense is dissolving even as I watch

Face

Here's my face slung on its bones like a slop
of concrete here the eyes punched into the mortar
hardened it seems to something like stone

this is my secret face seen only I like to believe
from within no one not even an all-seeing something
could perceive its true semblance visible solely

to me yet I suspect that sometimes and not
really rarely someone regarding my face will know
what's going on inside it know exactly

its fear or fretful confusion while I keep insisting
I don't believe I'm feeling such things
how could I why would I cling to them but

face if I splayed a hand on you to more closely
conceal your this and your that would I know
what everyone else does of my foreboding?

First Dying

He thought he knew dying the near edge
of dying because everything was so taxing
every moment more taxing because waking

was taxing because rising from his chair
too taxing so it seemed reasonable to sprawl
on the reliable chair and because he was this tired

he thought he must know the onset of dying
the lurch into dying the first task of dying
did he think this had something to do with dying

believing his duty now was surrender
did he dare think dying was submission
to conditions not wholly unfamiliar dying might

be not even unpleasant he'd think even
lifting yourself on your flimsy legs to be blown
about in blind time like a guttering flame

Names

Inserted into my mouth my veins the repulsive
fat on my belly my many medications
slide through me into my blood and bones

like battalions of ax-wielding thugs slashing
stabbing shrinking this engorging that
strong enough to tunnel through tissues

known hitherto only to matters of life
as *inner being* each drug with its own
mythic name a stinking shaman might burp

in consonant grunts and lung farts the rattle
and groans of his convulsionist dancing awing
the helpless patient who lies eyes stapled open

seeing nothing and mute as the excrement
of the corpse he'll have become shuddering
as it's kicked into the ditch back of the hut

You

Always beside me always so closely to me
that you might be within me or be me
especially that night I couldn't breathe

then you were emphatically with me
I saw you there not gasping with
me as I gasped but radiant with hope

though hope's such an insignificant
term compared to the panic barely suppressed
I couldn't help seeing in your eyes

as you waited and I couldn't help either
not allowing death to enter the drama
because that might undo you and I needed

you even just from that side of my life
even defined by your valiant hope and
being your self in a way I'd never before known

Tasks

Every gesture a task a chore not in the old
domestic sense of cherished duties
but rather purposeless acts their only aim

distraction from interminable demanding
mortality stuff but might my hypothetical
dying still concealed in and from me demand

even more attention than I'd have thought
especially in those abysses beneath mind
where unclear obligations demand command

but leave gaps in which taskless time swells
with too many left over hours to come to terms with
for isn't dwelling on self even part of the time

a waste for dwelling even part-time in those depths
is futile and to escape requires more effortful
toil than there's energy in the world for

Really

This is really happening this is really
not merely my death drawing closer
but the messy undomesticated sprawl

of thought which all but the most fortunate
have to go through here the indignities
degradations anything that might be left

of self-cultivation swiped away and then
you know it might be this day
when you'll be reduced to the outposts

of mind scattered through the corporeal
self and the facts of the flesh
you can no longer regulate or contain

all loosening turning to pathos and grief
and why is this happening you want to ask
while knowing the answer isn't to be borne

Eyes

When I close my eyes or I should say when
my eyes close because I don't will them to close
they decide despite me and they close

and to open them have them working again
I have to come up with a *reason* unlike when
they clicked and flew open as soon as they shut

unless I'd closed them for sleep or love or to keep
myself from being afraid while now being
behind my closed lids is more than seductive

it's normal and along with it the temptation keeps
taking me why not stay why not let myself stay
here so that other unspeakable thought-thing I dare

not confront might not take me and how not believe
if I were to stay here behind this veil the appalling
truth wouldn't when it arrived surprise me at all

Bone

And my bones and my living flesh turning
to stone how will they manage their fusion
how will I be brought as every being

must be sooner or later to its inevitable
transformation its passing from unending
to ending when time is once again a canal

like that through which our eruption into
the selves that exalt and suffer clutched us
will there be fractures in the suddenly

vulnerable precarious systems do we end
as tangles of molecules slashing ourselves
like the tails of comets until we cry out

if we could only deceive death reach into
the mechanism and stop it just dial
the swiveling switch so it would read *off*

Old

Look at him sidling like some sub-terrestrial
some broken down predator-prey thing fear-
bitten hate-bitten furtively drifting among others

like him though he's invisible to them he likes
to believe because so like them this spy in his time-
woven depths impotently trying to forgive

the weaknesses of his own tremulous vessel
trying to lift itself in his slackness his softness
on its crook of his spine believing he might enact

a concealment unsullied by terror always the spy
espies endings not only others' but its terrible
own not only those it imagines trying to lift

themselves from despondencies like his own
his repugnant humiliation how courageous these
others manifesting no mortification like his

Symptoms

What a vile word sharing as it does the trivia
of cough or sniffle yet which makes me ask
(furtively of my own rarely candid body)

if I feel more ill than I did last week
is my breath coming shorter when I try
to walk is what feels like the petty onset

of a dismissible fever or flu really
a portion of a definitely greater menace
a vessel let's say that blithely takes you

and your breath in and breath out
and with no drama at all turns them
into *conditions* which must be reflected

upon in different modes of attention but
from which you're helpless to effect a peace
you might someday turn onto yourself

Secrets

If I keep secret from you that I'm spinning
if I don't hint to you I feel I'm falling
if I keep hidden from you that I'm fainting

the next death-thing wants on its own
to say I'm expiring or on the way to expiring
not expiring in itself but in some strange way

close to or even adjacent to it but there's no
reason that sharing with you the spinning
should evoke a premonition of expiring

still certain I am I'm far from any kind
of extinction can you hear that can you
and I hear that waking together in which

I'm not 'spinning' my head not 'turning'
I'm only waiting as everything must for its
long-concealed turnings to be revealed

Labor

Of the dictator of some far off country
the news speaks of his medical team that
for several years has been *fighting for his life*

which makes me wonder not without a slash
of anxiety if that's what's been going on
here whether my doctors there are so many

are laboring if that's the word do doctors
actually labor not just to make me stronger
with more stamina etc to keep me going

keep me going unsettling thought
though it's surely a more realistic way
to consider my relatively animated condition

as matter being *fought for* a wild
something to be tamed and retrained
such resistance it has though such power

Rays

Fresco of spear-fighting Etruscans or Greeks
or some army anyway with its marvelous armor
but some warriors despite those invulnerable plates

have sharp spears thrust into them and on through
into the painted air just as radiation blasts through us
though not in my friend's mind whose doctor

referred to his x-ray apparatus as a 'spot welder'
which for some reason elated my friend gave him
hope though like much hope it didn't work out

in the end for even a spot welder no matter
how heartening its name how glowing its promise
knows well as it buzzes and clanks its limits

and those who promise me many fine bodily
outcomes without ever precisely specifying what
are they also merely too confident gunners?

Better

When I'm feeling 'better' that's to say
closer to 'normal' there's a veering in my sense
of being who I am and used to be

the template for myself has radically shifted
and links me with a vision that's gone awry
out of sync I'm out of sync that is to say

with the apparatus within my self I used to
and assumed I'd always spin my webs in
a conception of myself that had certain

boundaries edges however out of focus
in which I'd always move instead of this half-
healed structure which has become the ultimate

of who I am and will be as I wander
through some dimension where I breathe
I think easier then know after I don't

Rage

Long time since rage groundless anger
engulfed me for no nameable reason with
no apparent actual cause but itself its own

frustration fury that makes me want to destroy
no matter what to assuage the anger
I feel towards my affliction and if I don't act

on it now some great part of my world
will forever be unsatisfied unconsummated
though what can that possibly infer

is there a fury equal to the robe of illness
that encases me as though in an embrace
composed itself of raging resentment

and hastened by still being able to contain
enough of me in itself to crush me
and dissolve me in my own wrath

Impatience

Get it over with's not what Adam would
have shouted to serpent when his going began
not *get me out of here get me over with*

never *is more likely what he'd have groaned*
unlike that chip of me that petrifies
not daring to postulate any sort of departure

but keeps anyway telling itself over and over
not like begging to oh I don't know pick
your king your old god get this over with

you would say pull up this halfway death
finish this endless non-suffering suffering
release me though I don't really mean it

for wouldn't I have to tear myself to leave
my beloved and wouldn't my beloved be torn
too and isn't it intolerable to entertain that?

My Double

Not Nabokov's Dostoevsky's Poe's
of the whole crew no one remotely like mine
who regards me across a clinic's abyss

non-existence enveloping him while his
proximity to it makes him glow in the sheenless
warship grey of his skin the crushed slump

of his shoulders the glance he flings at me
I realize I'm meant to take as a challenge
because he knows his knowledge cowers in me

and because even now much later his presence
alive only in vaults of memory where we circle
each other in the accusing field of his glare

I know what he sees is gullible hope and
that he'd condemned me for all I'd perceived
in him and refused to allow in myself

What

I keep asking myself something
but what is it I ask what is it that tugs
so slow-wittedly and lethargically

that it seems to pay no attention to me
what is it that plods through me like the oldest
mule in creation and if there were still flies

from that ancient world it would be covered
with them but would hardly notice twitching
its slack hide only enough not to be wholly

consumed as cicadas in myths are consumed
by their singing and what is it in me that's
being consumed and what would *consumed* mean

to be made to vanish or cease to exist
but what part of me could ever vanish cease
to exist without me even as I know it still does

Worse

It seems my fear has outwitted me again
changed its costume sharpened its knives
come back out of its hiding place crept

behind me where I can't picture it
but can only sense its presence so can't
steel myself the way I could so well

such a short time ago and pretend though
knowing I was that it wasn't there
it's come upon me so deviously this time

I have to know I'm mortal as I'd always
been but back then I could think I'd possessed
such a small portion of eternity I'd hardly remark

when I'd consumed it while now all pretexts
are gone leaving me not as I was when fear
first came upon me but wretchedly worse

How Many

How many times do I find myself
whispering *later* even as I have to grasp
death's advent will have to bring *sooner*

does this happen to us all I wonder
I mean all of us not only threatened
but who have our ending laid before us

all of us all whom death has been given
and the word death which the world
was so eager to have us know

so that now just saying it seems almost
a kind of vengeance just to be able to utter
later later and find some sustenance

some surcease in the uttering itself
in the silent insistent sob that finds
its way out in futile blurts *later later*

Friends

Those of you who've gone before how precious
you remain how little your essential nature
has altered and insofar as it has I can't grasp

how you might be other than you ever were
surely you aren't wholly 'gone' though that's
undeniably your essence now to have gone

surely you haven't even metaphorically risen
or descended it's just that you're not *available*
to those left behind unavailable for what

except the generation of future memories
I don't know that's the painful aspect of love
gone to no longer generate memories to share

here we laughed here danced all falls away
only the tattered snatches of what we call past
echo out from the isolate provinces of time

Fine

I'm fine I like to proclaim I'm doing just
fine is what I do claim everything's excellent
working better than could be hoped

everyone's optimistic I repeat and repeat
except what I don't claim or not aloud
is that my ending has arrived in a new way

I mean the end I've lived through more
than a few times real dying other diseases
pneumonia car wrecks all of that crap

but this time the dying I've lived with these
many decades seem enfolded or crushed in me
and is merely waiting patiently waiting

for it and my cringing body to choose
the month hour second which when it arrives
I'll only know but here upon me it will be

The Past

Whence come these granite memories
of myself as thoughtless selfish self-centered
beyond what even the term might imply

whence this spoiled child grasping teenager
covetous young then older then old adult
and why now when I'm almost choking

with such acid memories this obsessive
not letting go these what feel like inept
repentances all frantically boiling in me

then steaming away concentrated and
distilled into an indistinguishable mass
or clot rather find the lowest word lowest

lump of memory yes that only can hope
to be rescued from the sludge and scum
of foolish wrongs that endure and endure

Everyone

I fancy everyone I've ever known well
or not in one space a hall perhaps a tent
great flapper stretched over the patch

of the earth of my life so I can count to myself
the friends the unfriends even the lovers
from that awful wonderful time of lovers

who could be called such only in looking back
let them be here too in that mortal-immortal
where we swarm on each other embracing

and where I lower my face lightly to yours
offering shy kisses not for memories of loss
or regret but because of my yearning to revel

again in those moments I squandered that left me
friend-self enemy-self with so many memories
still cunningly waiting their revealment

Here

Am I here I ask ask again am I still *here*
though I'm not certain whom I'm asking
or what I'm still looking for out there

through the uncertain veils that descend
on my eyes clouds storm-clouds sky clearing
clouding or storming but though I know

I'm perceiving I'm struck by if not doubt
then by a question without meaning
a vacancy or some sort of *need* before

am I here comes again with its implication
I don't know though I'm aware I'm still
in a *life* or some other partly used realm

but still don't know how being with you
should feel free still certain something's here
in this broken light for no reason I inhabit

Coward

That's a word a term a notion a concept
a hook that sticks in your craw *coward*
cowardly weep you are and you know it

what are you moaning about voice my voice
perceiving that our planet is mortal and soon
will cry itself off some edge of non-being

but that you won't be there with your children
and grand and those so many others you love
not be there find surcease in avoidance escape

not be there thank you dear death *not be there*
darling death that will scrape me away from
my grief for the world like a slate erased

and float me off without having an earth to console
without me isn't it a relief to think *without me*
so as not to have to cry again *oh wounded earth*

Wounded Earth

Is it as I suspect not that rare for you to be
wounded ravaged stripped of so much
of what you wore with seeming pride

your seething glittering oceans your forests
nothing new for you meteors comets
volcanoes extinctions the battering ice ages

so perhaps we shouldn't psalm *poor earth*
for truly we moan and despair for ourselves
cast into that future we dread while the time

in which we sorrowed you'll not have regretted
because how can earth not have a past
and how can earth even with a past so fouled

not notice how we departed leaving our heirs
to mourn this patch this sherd of existence
we'd been so confident we'd cherish forever

Embrace

This once I don't know and can't guess
why it should be this once when we come
together bring our bodies together

your arms round my neck my arms
round your waist this once there's a poignancy
to our embrace this once there's a kind

of not desperation but force a force
that takes us both and presses us against
each other more than 'presses' hurls us

each to and against the other in a way we've
never experienced before and I can't tell if
it represents or embodies a recognition

of mortality a premonition of what will be
coming to take us or whether this is beyond
us beyond what's coming to us beyond all

Bad Day

Stagger is something I'd never noticed myself
doing or it would be better to say have done to me
stagger a bit because my legs have gone weak

lurch sway totter not totter please bad enough
to have to clutch a banister grab a railing
without accusing myself of being more feeble

than I am then to sit reeling on the edge
of my bed falling weakly onto its expanse
then struggling to haul my head to the pillow

to verify whether I'm breathing as I should
if my heart is beating as it should not lurching
stumbling trembling and if my sight's clear

despite the innards of my eyes being worn
by their trying to peek past the dreadful edge
of a precipice to a future I didn't know was there

The Heart

Catch your breath as though under water but
in my shell I still can't catch my breath or
my life all keeps being stripped off to reveal

a victim then a victim beneath and each time
catch your breath indicates someone *marooned
in his heart* but then it's not any longer either

by itself or even a *self* my longer as I used
to know victimless self *catch your breath*
it's all being taken away lost breath lost self

and what sort of pathetic self vanishes
under so little pressure stress and duress
surely the self beneath this one has more

strength more power than *catch your breath*
but no the sheer fright the sudden onset
of it all *catch your breath* the fear of it all

Lonely

How strange to be lonely one day and not
the next when I remember so clearly
how the passion not to be lonely was the enduring

need of my first life the illusion that being
alone would injure me wound me neutralize me
leave me with no actual ego I could believe in

then how long after would it have been came
the realization that the most acute moments
of solitude were in the company of others

it didn't matter loved ones or not only a few
a frightening few you most of all brought
respite and this is surely redundant presence

a presence that effused around us joining us
bringing us closer touching or not so now
the thought of leaving you alone tears so

Begun Again

Are you ready I ask myself am I ready
like echoes of an echo it keeps throbbing
are you ready and things dim are you well

prepared and things brighten again and in
their brightening sadly unprepare me
leave me out here myself once alone

yet so harshly unalone so suddenly abrasively
with so many my love for one before the rest
but still so many so many close and closer

and it's the start again it's once again the onset
and beginning it's the reimagining of so many
different endings all of which find an end

in which sorrowfully I'm alone but taking
portions of these others with me if only I could
truly go alone be alone would I find peace?

Can It Be Lost?

I seem to have forgotten death or my death
it's no longer within around upon me
not that I truly believe it's gone from me

but rather that it's permitted itself
to retract from the part of me that ruminates
or feels or gives credence or anything else

so I'm here now without it but the feeling is
I'm with nothing I'm no longer encased
or covered or lined I'm just here not waiting

its return surely not that but still a bereft
feeling of being in and containing a space
a state of non-life so I know death's gone

having taken a lobe of my mortal awareness
along with it and there's something else
I can't name or reach out to for it's taken too

Trees

I'd almost forgotten but haven't that stand
of great trees at the edge of a pond beneath
which I stood with you one morning in rain

and felt something I might have called bliss
or if not bliss then something of a new light
that stripped away portions of my anxieties

like excess garments unseasonable cloaks
as though I could actually denude myself
because you and these presences would protect me

and I must have called out to you to protect me
and everything else around me as I stood there
in the actual world protect me in the serenity

of the inconceivable volume these titanic trunks
and you with them protect me make me fearless
in a way I could never be before you without you

Crying

What are they *for* these dribbles these drops
what do they *do* that some other body work
some simpler less theatrical reflex wouldn't

from that first amazingly unreasonable spank
for some long forgotten offense sin affront
which soils us or no leaves us somehow *marked*

within our deepest heart with weakness
cowardness all the labels we accumulate
and nail into ourselves leaving gaps rips

openings to the world we didn't mean to have
and you wish you were someone else
someone unlike us constructed of tubes

of fear or sadness that dip into the secret
wells of misery lakes oceans of angst
and then the overflow only then tears

Others

Sometimes others' going numbs me
I mean others I know and admired once
they're here then going then vanished

and the pain I assumed I'd feel is uncertain
vague spread out thinly over many months
even years it evades me I'm here without

this other I loved yet there's no puncture
in the ordinary opening and closing of attention
and even the pain of no pain isn't given to me

I'm belittled trivialized before myself for this
thing that doesn't capture or enwrap me
this complex I used to call *grief* but can't

now which makes me incidental to myself
and everything else as though I've already lost
all but this labyrinth of numb disorder

Air

Not air as on that island the weeks of love's onset
not air even on those mornings with mild
waves insinuating themselves on the shore

we looked out on nor the cypress intensifying
the scent of the breezes nor the breezes themselves
but a medium rather of hidden arcane qualities

such was the air in the first days of illness
enfolding me in a texture I'd never known
as though in another genre of simple being

something I'd not merely bring into my lungs
but capture and devour so pure was it
so definitive as it churned so powerfully

through me so I'd wonder if the part of me
that was me knew already how precious air
soon would become and remain glorious air

Depression

I'm learning or rather I'm being instructed
in depression not only depression as I usually
define it as a sadness that wraps you in it

but rather in the more insidious I'd almost
say gentle melancholy *gentle* as in love faded
love lost through what I'm calling depression

there's no love object no love absence nothing
without or within to center your emotions
you're just alone with a feeling that isn't

real feeling yet drags at you making its own
lack of definition the very substance of anything
you can think of except the worst part is that

you know what you're doing now isn't thinking
you're just emptying yourself leaving only
enough of you to care if you might still exist

Day Off

Unfamiliar silence within deeper silence
soothing sheltering heartening subtracting
hours that don't succumb except to themselves

and to you and as though from another fear
another forgiving of fear though now it seems
never to need or want that slice of anguish

rather only this inexplicable moment of peace
which I thought I'd never have needed here
in my list of unscrambled sorrow but here

it is needed again still partly calming one
hour then another seemingly needing
even torn away from a lost remembrance

still I'm here unworn untendered with you
held with you in a calm I never realized
I was capable of that even now fades and goes out

Against Me

I find myself talking to death *talking*
aloud asking questions in my real voice
I'm sure I don't actually expect answers

just some partial acknowledgements
I imagine of the sort people of faith feel
when they envisage earth shuddering

sky breaking that great gale of credence
except I don't need such unsubtle responses
puffed up show-offy instead I murmur to death

as though it had intruded invisibly into my flesh
pressing against me tightly though without pain
as I offer up this or that question or complaint

silent death hangs slackly faded bare
I feel against me with abiding terror
as it offers my own ignorance to mock me

Lord Death

As though death this time was speaking
aloud *ah you're here again* death murmurs
this time it's you longing towards and for me

while I'm refusing to hear you as I well can
for it's not for you or anything living to share
in the dimensions of your stay here

and your going your being here and having
been here and then not for the not
becomes as though never and even as though

too is a lie and are and were lies too and
that's what you'll have learned or will soon
and what else can be taught other than that

therefore I spurn you disdain ignore you
but you'll hardly know that all you'll know
is that you know nothing of me or yourself

Life

Always now the word the idea the very notion
resides lavishly in the past where it once
meant dread fear all the dire forebodings

of those fearful vacuums that carried with them
intimations of destruction finalities ending
while now *life* can indicate things salvaged

as though the most fleeting of feelings
could be held could be contained could
be experienced at will or again or just once

as though one might close one's eyes and
chant *life* or as though one might gaze up out
of the world and hold it in memory like a poem

here I am the poem would begin take me keep me
but how do we keep you when we need you
only when by definition you'll be gone

Whenever

Whenever it will be it will be *now*
its *own* now that I'm aware will have left
particles in the past as a new galaxy dusts

the universe with its spinning constituents
helium carbon as well as those other
elements received directly disbelief terror

awe as always before the continuing fact
of endless existence in which you will no longer
participate except in this appalling *now*

mind-borne tentacles stretched back
across this blinding cloud this dust of despair
or not despair simply *knowing* the *now*

will be upon me and tear me away from
so much I long for as though it were gone
already into thrashing memory for it has

Farewell

I want to wish you goodbye but don't dare
essential it is to wish you goodbye farewell
thank you acknowledge how you devised

a life for me I never imagined I'd have
but saying goodbye can seem a diminishing
a subtraction something that must never

be thought though it already has been
and will be again but never allowed to reach
the lips to pass into the realm of language

or come too clearly even into the mind
the mind so sadly vulnerable with its capacity
for contradicting itself yet there must be

a way to cry goodbye aloud to leave you
these inadequate thanks without resorting
to rending farewell oh dear heart farewell

C.K. Williams (1936-2015) was born in New Jersey, and lived latterly in Paris, Normandy and Princeton. He published a dozen books in Britain with Bloodaxe, including *New & Selected Poems* (1995), *The Vigil* (1997), *Repair* (1999) and *The Singing* (2003) – all four of these were Poetry Book Society Recommendations – followed by *Collected Poems* (2006), *Wait* (2010), *Writers Writing Dying* (2013), another Poetry Book Society Recommendation, and the posthumously published *Falling Ill* (2017). *All at Once: Prose Poems* (2014) and *Selected Later Poems* (2015) were published by Farrar, Straus and Giroux in the US.

Flesh and Blood won the National Book Critics Circle Prize in 1987, *Repair* was awarded the 2000 Pulitzer Prize, and *The Singing* won the National Book Award for 2003. He was also honoured with the Ruth Lilly Poetry Prize, the PEN Voelker Career Achievement Award in Poetry for 1998; a Guggenheim Fellowship, two NEA grants, the Berlin Prize of the American Academy in Berlin, a Lila Wallace Fellowship, and prizes from PEN and the American Academy of Arts and Letters.

He published a memoir, *Misgivings* (Farrar, Straus and Giroux), in 2000, which was awarded the PEN Albrand Memoir Award, and translations of Sophocles' *Women of Trachis*, Euripides' *Bacchae*, and poems of Francis Ponge, among others. He published two books of essays, *Poetry and Consciousness* (University of Michigan Press, 1998), and *In Time: Poets, Poems, and the Rest* (University of Chicago Press, 2012), and his book on Walt Whitman, *On Whitman* (Princeton University Press), appeared in 2010.

He taught in the Creative Writing Program at Princeton University, and was a chancellor of the Academy of American Poets.